THE SEVEN SORROWS

of the

BLESSED VIRGIN MARY

Poems in Honor

of

Our Lady of Sorrows

by

Donna Sue Berry

Edited by Eugenia L. Zanone

Berry Books Publishing

Acknowledgement

To my sweet husband, Doc, thank you for your incredible love and support in getting my poems together and creating our first book! You are the most amazing gift from God, and I love you.

To my two girls, Crystal and Melanie, these poems are for you. I thank you for always loving and encouraging me to follow the dream of publishing a book of my poetry. I love you.

To my dear Mamma, who read my very first poems that I scribbled onto notebook paper when I was in high school. You always hugged and told me that they were the best! I know you will carry this little book around in your purse that very rarely leaves your arm. I love you so much.

ISBN 978-0-692-95260-3

Dedicated
to
Our Lady of Sorrows

THE PROMISES

The Blessed Virgin Mary revealed promises to St. Bridget of Sweden (1303-1373) that if her devotees would daily pray seven Hail Marys, while meditating on her seven sorrows or dolors, and tears, that they would receive these graces:

1. "I will grant peace to their families."

2. "They will be enlightened about the Divine Mysteries."

3. "I will console them in their pains, and I will accompany them in their work."

4. "I will give them as much as they ask for as long as it does not oppose the adorable will of my Divine Son or the sanctification of their souls."

5. "I will defend them in their spiritual battles with the infernal enemy, and I will protect them at every instant of their lives.

6. "I will visibly help them at the moment of their death – they will see the face of their mother."

7. "I have obtained this grace from my divine Son, that those who propagate this devotion to my tears and dolors, will be taken directly from this earthly life to eternal happiness, since all their sins will be forgiven and my Son will be their eternal consolation and joy."

Table of Contents

Devotion to Our Lady of Sorrows is as old as that moment when Saint Simeon announced to the Blessed Mother that a sword would pierce her soul. There she stood, holding her new born baby, Jesus, in the temple where He had just been circumcised according to Jewish law, and she quite possibly heard him cry out in pain. It would be the first time that He would shed His Precious Blood. At that moment, the Blessed Mother went from the extreme joy of presenting her Son to God in the temple, to the depths of sorrow as she foresaw his suffering and death.

Our Lady's First Sorrow

The Prophecy of Simeon

O Simeon, O Simeon, what prompted you to say,

Those sad words you spoke to Mary, which made her cry that day?

When you saw the Virgin Mother, with Jesus her new born,

Did you perceive the bloody Cross, Nails, and the Crown of Thorns?

As she climbed upon the temple steps, was your soul set on fire?

Could you hear the loud "Hosannas" sung by an angel choir?

Then lifting him into your arms according to the law,

Was it the Lord Almighty in the tiny face you saw?

Did her joy turn into sorrow as you talked about the Lord,

And how someday she'd suffer with her soul pierced by a sword?

But as they turned and walked away, did it become quite clear,

Our sins would nail him to that cross and cause our Lady's tears?

Our Lady's Second Sorrow

The Flight into Egypt

"Arise and take the baby
To Egypt with his mother,
Fly far from here, and don't look back,
But travel undercover."

As the Angel spoke to Joseph,
He woke him from his rest,
He warned him of the peril to
The babe at Mary's breast.

Though Joseph saw the danger in
What lay for them ahead.
He knew that if they stayed behind
His son would soon be dead.

So that night they left for Egypt,
No one knew that they had gone.
No one knew that they were fleeing,
Long before the break of dawn.

He quickly took his family,
Far from their holy home,
Far from their Jewish culture and
The lives which they had known.

Into a land they'd never seen,
So full of history.
Into the Land of Pharaoh where
God set the Hebrews free.

There Saint Joseph would protect them,
With angels by his side,
And live in humble poverty
Until King Herod died.

Our Lady's Third Sorrow

The Loss of the Child Jesus in the Temple

Mary's heart kept beating faster, her fear grew deeper, too.
But night turned into morning with still no son in view.
They'd searched all night through caravans, among family and
friends,
But couldn't find their Jesus, and they feared a tragic end.

St. Joseph said, "Let's turn around," their mood anxious and grim.
They started back toward the gate, back to Jerusalem.
Back to the crowded city streets, into the noisy crowd,
Her broken heart preparing her for Christ wrapped in a shroud.

They knew that soon the day would come when he would leave
this earth,
When all of it would come to light, things hidden since his birth.
But now she craved the sight of him, the sound of his young voice;
Back to the temple they would go, they had no other choice.

In temple then to their surprise, he sat among the men,
With doctors who were listening, who stood in awe of him.
"Son, why hast thou done so to us?" Pained words he heard her sigh.
Though she'd not understand at all, the words he'd then reply.

"How is it that you've sought me here?" Their confusion must
have shown. "I am about my Father's work,"
Yet he left with them for home.
Back in Nazareth, their holy home, he'd always honor them,
And there in wisdom grow with grace, before his God and men.

Our Lady's Fourth Sorrow

Mary Meets Jesus Carrying His Cross

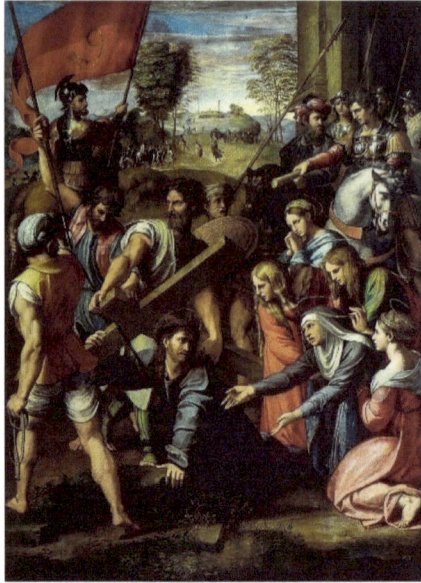

As she came around the corner,
She stopped to catch her breath,
Then through the crowd she saw his face,
His pallor quite like death.

Her heart almost exploded as
She then beheld her son,
With his bruised and battered body,
And the torture they had done.

He sunk beneath the heavy cross,
As legs gave way in pain.
A man of massive open wounds,
A lamb that'd soon be slain.

No way for her to get to him,
The soldiers like a wall,
Her ears assaulted by the din,
With horrid, cursing calls.

So, weakened by the loss of blood,
He seemed to stare in space.
But when she moved into his view,
He saw his Mother's face.

For just a moment they could see
Into each other's eyes.
Both felt the pain reflected there,
Each heard their silent cries.

O the thoughts that passed between them,
As soldiers pushed and shoved.
A son and mother sacrifice,
No two more ever loved.

But fleeting moments soon were gone,
They yanked him from her view,
And vanishing into the crowd,
She felt her pain renew.

Our Lady's Fifth Sorrow

The Crucifixion

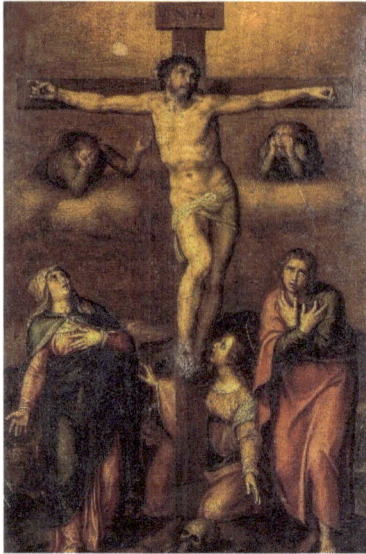

While you stood there in the chaos,
Could you see past all the pain?
Past the sword that ripped your soul,
To your son's triumphant reign?

Did the sands there of Golgotha
Scratch lines into your face,
Mixing with the blood of Jesus,
Dearest Lady, full of grace?

While you stayed beneath his shadow,
While he hung there on the cross,
Could you feel your own wounds bleeding,
As his blood fell to the rocks?

As the turmoil clutched your saddened soul,
Did your heart completely break?
Could you hear the soldier cursing
When his hammer hit the stake?

The *Prophecy of Simeon*,
Had it at last come true,
Where the thoughts of many people
Would lay bare because of you?

Was it when the earth was quaking
That reality set in,
Your son had died to save our souls,
Because of all our sin?

I ask you all these questions as
I'm leading up to one.
Can you forgive me, Blessed Mother,
For the dying of your son?

Our Lady's Sixth Sorrow

Mary Receives the Body of Jesus from the Cross

Had it really been that long ago she'd held him in her arms,
And kissed his tiny tear stained face until his heart grew calm?
But now they sat in darkness on a hill they called the Skull,
Where she kissed his bruised and lifeless face, its pallor gray
and dull.

She had known this day was coming, for she'd known it was God's
plan,
That he'd grow up to shed his blood, a sacrificial lamb.
But knowing lessened not the pain, nor quelled her trembling hands,
As she held his body close to hers, her son, God's son made man.

'Oh, sad and sorrowing Mother, your soul pierced by a sword,
It was our sins that killed your son, we crucified our Lord.
Forgive us, now the time has come to lay him in the grave.
We take away your very all. It was your all you gave.'

Our Lady's Seventh Sorrow

The Body of Jesus is Placed in The Tomb

Now Sabbath was upon them,
And the air began to chill.
Their tiny group moved quickly as
They started down the hill.

The horror of his sacrifice,
The blood, the nails, and tears,
Would stay with them forever,
To haunt them through the years.

As Joseph offered a new tomb,
Wherein to place her son,
They wrapped him in a linen cloth,
Quite hurried to be done.

But standing there his mournful Mother,
Stayed present 'til the end.
Though weight from her great sorrow made
Her weary shoulders bend.

Such pain no one has ever known,
As she who gave him birth.
No grief, no sorrow, quite like hers,
Never upon the earth.

With strength, she conquered her desire
To stay within his tomb.
Was grace that prompted her away,
Back to the upper room.

Beside her John and Magdalene,
Not leaving her alone,
But in sadness moved in silence,
While walking Mary home.

Traditional Prayers

to

Our Lady of Sorrows

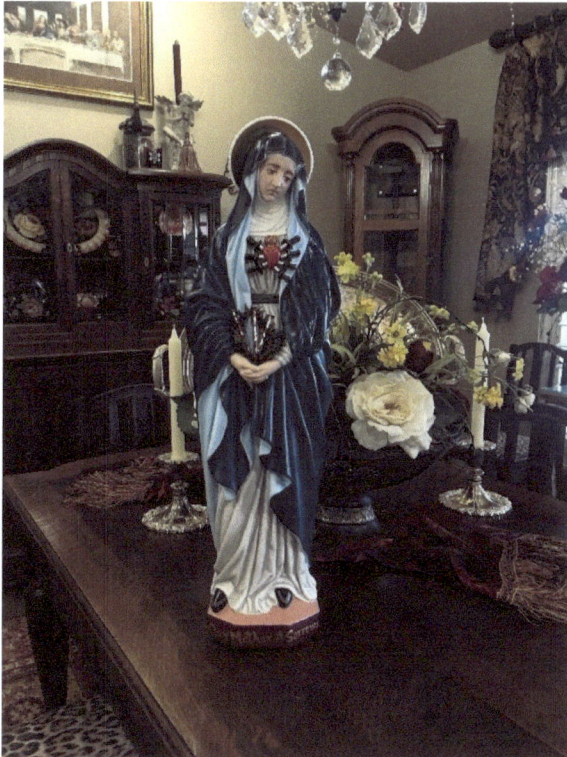

"Holy Mother, pierce me through,
in my heart each wound renew, of my Savior crucified."

Litany of Our Lady of Seven Sorrows

Lord, have mercy on us.
Christ, have mercy on us.
Lord, have mercy on us.
Christ, hear us.
Christ, graciously hear us.
God the Father of heaven, *have mercy on us.*
God the Son, Redeemer of the world, *have mercy on us.*
God the Holy Spirit, *have mercy on us.*
Holy Trinity, one God, *have mercy on us.*
Holy Mother of God, *pray for us.*
Holy Virgin of virgins, *pray for us.*
Mother crucified, *pray for us.*
Mother sorrowful, *pray for us.*
Mother tearful, *pray for us.*
Mother afflicted, *pray for us.*
Mother forsaken, *pray for us.*
Mother desolate, *pray for us.*
Mother bereft of thy Son, *pray for us.*
Mother pierced with a sword, *pray for us.*
Mother filled with anguish, *pray for us.*
Mother crucified in heart, *pray for us.*
Mother most sad, *pray for us.*
Fountain of tears, *pray for us.*
Mass of suffering, *pray for us.*
Mirror of Patience, *pray for us.*
Rock of consistency, *pray for us.*
Anchor of confidence, *pray for us.*
Refuge of the forsaken, *pray for us.*
Shield of the oppressed, *pray for us.*
Subduer of the unbelieving, *pray for us.*
Comfort of the wretched, *pray for us.*
Medicine of the sick, *pray for us.*
Strength of the weak, *pray for us.*
Harbor of the wrecked, *pray for us.*
Allay of tempests, *pray for us.*
Resource of mourners, *pray for us.*

Terror of the treacherous, *pray for us.*
Treasure of the faithful, *pray for us.*
Eye of the prophets, *pray for us.*
Staff of Apostles, *pray for us.*
Crown of martyrs, *pray for us.*
Light of Confessors, *pray for us.*
Pearl of Virgins, *pray for us.*
Consolation of widows, *pray for us.*
Joy of all Saints, *pray for us.*

Lamb of God, who takes away the sins of the world, *spare us, O Jesus.*
Lamb of God, who takes away the sins of the world, *graciously hear us, O Jesus.*
Lamb of God, who takes away the sins of the world, *have mercy on us, O Jesus.*

Look down upon us, *deliver us from all trouble in the power of Jesus Christ. Amen.*

Imprint, O Lady, thy wound upon my heart, that I may read therein sorrow and love: sorrow, to endure every sorrow for thee; love, to despise every love for thee.

Virgin most sorrowful, pray for us.

Virgo dolorsissima, ora pro nobis.

Prayers to the Sorrowful Mother
(from the Raccolta)

Mary, most holy Virgin and Queen of Martyrs, accept the sincere homage of my filial affection. Into thy heart, pierced by so many swords, do thou welcome my poor soul. Receive it as the companion of thy sorrows at the foot of the Cross, on which Jesus died for the redemption of the world. With thee, O Sorrowful Virgin, I will gladly suffer all the trials, contradictions, and infirmities which it shall please Our Lord to send me. I offer them all to thee in memory of thy sorrows, so that every thought of my mind, and every beat of my heart may be an act of compassion and of love for thee. And do thou, sweet Mother, have pity on me, reconcile me to thy divine Son Jesus, keep me in His grace and assist me in my last agony, so that I may be able to meet thee in Heaven and sing thy glories. Amen.

Most holy Virgin and Mother, whose soul was pierced by a sword of Sorrow in the Passion of thy Divine Son, and Who in His Glorious Resurrection was filled with never-ending joy at His triumph; obtain for us who call upon thee, so to be partakers in the adversities of Holy Church and the sorrows of the Sovereign Pontiff, as to be found worthy to rejoice with them in the consolations for which we pray, in charity and peace of the same Christ our Lord. Amen.

(Written by Pope Pius X)

Chaplet of Our Lady's Seven Sorrows

O my God, I am heartily sorry for having offended Thee, and I detest all my sins because I dread the loss of Heaven and the pains of hell; but most of all because they offend Thee my God, Who art all good and deserving of all my love. I firmly resolve with the help of Thy grace to confess my sins, to do penance, and to amend my life. Amen.

V. O God, come to my assistance,
R. O Lord, make haste to help me.

Glory be to the Father, to the Son, and to the Holy Ghost. As it was in the beginning, is now, and ever shall be, world without end. Amen.

Say three *Hail Marys* in honor of the tears of the Blessed Mother. Announce the Sorrow and then pray a Hail Mary.

1. The First Sorrow - The Prophecy of Simeon – Hail Mary . . .

2. The Second Sorrow - The Flight into Egypt – Hail Mary . . .

3. The Third Sorrow - Loss of Jesus in the Temple – Hail Mary. . .

4. The Fourth Sorrow - Meeting of Mary and Jesus on the Way to Calvary - Hail Mary . . .

5. The Fifth Sorrow- The Crucifixion and Death of Jesus- Hail Mary. . .

6. The Sixth Sorrow - Piercing of the Side of Jesus, and laying him in the arms of his Mother- Hail Mary . . .

7. The Seventh Sorrow – The Burial of Jesus - Hail Mary . . .

Novena to Our Lady of Sorrows
(from the Raccolta)

May be said as a nine-day novena and/or as a companion to the daily recitation of 7 Hail Marys offered in honor of Our Lady's Sorrows.

Leader: O God, come to my assistance;

Response: O Lord, make haste to help me.

Leader: Glory be to the Father, to the Son, and to the Holy Ghost.

Response: As it was in the beginning, is now and ever shall be, world without end. Amen.

Day 1. I grieve for thee, O Mary most sorrowful, in the affliction of thy tender heart at the prophecy of the holy and aged Simeon. Dear Mother, by thy heart so afflicted, obtain for me the virtue of humility and the Gift of the Holy Fear of God. *Pray one Hail Mary.*

Day 2. I grieve for thee, O Mary most sorrowful, in the anguish of thy most Affectionate heart during the flight into Egypt and thy sojourn there. Dear Mother, by thy heart so troubled, obtain for me the virtue of generosity, especially towards the poor, and the Gift of Piety. *Pray one Hail Mary.*

Day 3. I grieve for thee, O Mary most sorrowful, in those anxieties which tried thy troubled heart at the loss of thy dear Jesus. Dear Mother, by thy heart so full of anguish, obtain for me the virtue of chastity and the Gift of Knowledge. *Pray one Hail Mary.*

Day 4. I grieve for thee, O Mary most sorrowful, in the consternation of thy heart at meeting Jesus as He carried His Cross. Dear Mother, by thy heart so troubled, obtain for me the virtue of patience and the Gift of Fortitude. *Pray one Hail Mary.*

Day 5. I grieve for thee, O Mary most sorrowful, in the martyrdom which thy generous heart endured in standing near Jesus in His agony. Dear Mother, by thy heart afflicted in such wise, obtain for me the virtue of temperance and the Gift of Counsel. *Pray one Hail Mary.*

Day 6. I grieve for thee, O Mary most sorrowful, in the wounding of thy compassionate heart, when the side of Jesus was struck by the lance, and His heart was pierced. Dear Mother, by thy heart thus transfixed, obtain for me the virtue of fraternal charity and the Gift of Understanding. *Pray one Hail Mary.*

Day 7. I grieve for thee, O Mary most sorrowful, for the pangs that wrenched thy most loving heart at the burial of Jesus. Dear Mother, by thy heart sunk in the bitterness of desolation, obtain for me the virtue of diligence and the Gift of Wisdom. *Pray one Hail Mary.*

Leader: Pray for us, O Virgin most sorrowful,

Response: That we may be made worthy of the promises of Christ.

Let us pray

Let intercession be made for us, we beseech Thee, O Lord Jesus Christ, now and at the hour of our death, before the throne of Thy mercy, by the Blessed Virgin, Thy Mother, whose most holy soul was pierced by a sword of sorrow in the hour of Thy bitter Passion. We ask this through Thee, Jesus Christ, Savior of the world, who with the Father and the Holy Ghost livest and reignest world without end. Amen.

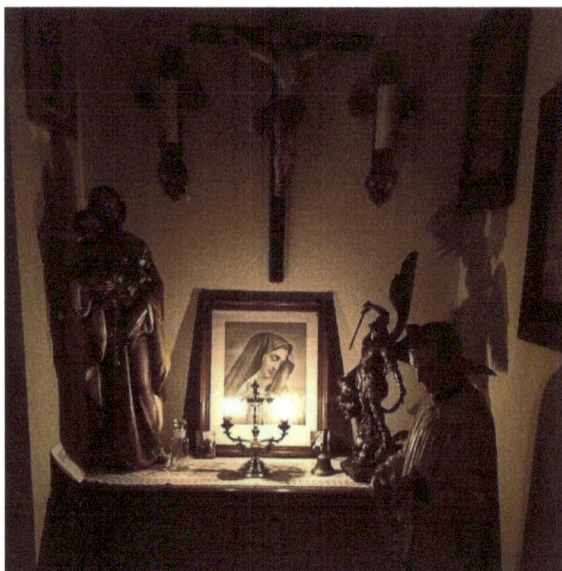

The Stabat Mater Dolorosa
(13th Century Marian Hymn
Ascribed to Jacopone Da Todi, O.F.M., d. 1306)

At the Cross her station keeping,
Stood the mournful Mother weeping,
While her Jesus hung above.

Through her heart, His sorrow sharing,
All His bitter anguish bearing,
Ran the sword of suffering love.

Oh, what sadness and affliction
Pressed that child of benediction,
Mother of the Holy One.

She who, bent in lamentation,
Saw the bitter desolation,
Of her well beloved son.

Who un-moved could see her languish,
See those tears of bitter anguish
Streaming down her tender cheek?

For her Child she saw dejected,
For His people's sins rejected,
And in bloody scourges rent.

Mournful Mother, let me borrow
Some of that most bitter sorrow,
Which for Jesus you did feel:

That my heart, new fervor gaining,
More devoted love attaining,
May to His pierced Heart appeal.

Mother, share with me your sorrow;
Let me of His torments borrow;
Print them on my sinful heart.

Since He wished to save me, dying,
Wounded in the Crucifying,
In His suffering give me part.

By the Cross of my salvation,
One with you in reparation,
May He all my sins forgive.

Virgin, all the saints exceeding,
Be not of my prayer unheeding;
Let me share with you your grief.

Be His wounds my consolation.
Be His Passion my salvation.
Be His dying my belief.

Christ, my Lord, in my last hour,
Grant that, through your Mother's power,
I may conquer every sin.

When my soul and body sever,
May I live with You forever,
To Your glory entering in. Amen.

Hail Holy Queen

Hail, Holy Queen, Mother of Mercy, Hail our life, our sweetness
and our hope. To thee do we cry, poor banished children of Eve. To
thee do we send up our sighs, mourning and weeping in this vale of
tears. Turn then, Most gracious Advocate, thine eyes of mercy
toward us, and after this our exile show unto us the blessed Fruit of
thy womb, Jesus, O Clement, O loving, O sweet
Virgin Mary.

V. Pray for us, O Holy Mother of God.
R. That we may be made worthy of the promises of Christ.

Holy Mother Church celebrates the Solemnity of Our Lady of Sorrows on September 15th, and the Friday of Passiontide is dedicated to her Seven Sorrows.

Works Cited

Picture of *Our Lady of Sorrows* found behind another framed picture which belonged to the author's great grandparents, Thomas and Margaret Stander.

Giotto, *Presentazione di Gesu Temio.* c.1304-1306. Fresco. Scrovegni (Arena) Chapel, Padua, Italy. www.the-athenaeum.org.

Botticelli, Sandro. *The Flight into Egypt.* c.1505. Museum Jacquemart-André, Paris. commons.wikimedia.org

Durer, Albrecht. *Christ Among the Doctors.* c.1506. Museo Thyssen-Bornemisza, Madrid, Spain. www.museothyssen.org

Raphael. *The Fall on the Road to Calvary*. c.1517. Museo del Prado, Madrid, Spain. https://en.wikipedia.org/wiki/Christ_Falling_on_the_Way_to_Calvary

Michelangelo. *Crucifixion*. c.1540. Rome, Italy. commons.wikimedia.org

Solari, Andrea. *Lamentation over the Dead Christ.* c. 1509. Musee du Louvre, Paris, France. https://commons.wikimedia.org/wiki/File:Andrea_Solario_-_Lamentation_over_the_Dead_Christ_-_WGA21603.jpg

Bassano, Francesco, the Younger. *Lamentation over the Dead Christ.* c.1580s. Private collection. https://commons.wikimedia.org/wiki/File:Francesco_Bassano_the_Younger_-_Lamentation_over_the_Dead_Christ_-_WGA01415.jpg

Schmalz, Herbert. *The Return from Calvary.* c.1891. Photo of painting taken at Yonderland in Mulhall, Oklahoma. http://yonderlandthewaystation.org/

Our Lady of Sorrows statue at Yonderland
in Mulhall, Oklahoma. 2017.
http://yonderlandthewaystation.org/about/.

Domestic altar. Private collection.

Statue of Our Lady of Sorrows at Yonderland.
Created by Heavenly Saints. https://www.etsy.com/shop/HeavenlySaints

About the Author

Born and raised in central Oklahoma, USA, Donna Sue Berry is a wife, mother of two, and grandmother of twelve. She and retired rancher husband, Joel Doc, share their time between the wheat fields of Oklahoma and the mountains of Montana. Donna Sue began writing poetry and song lyrics soon after she first read Romeo and Juliet during her junior year in high school. However, it wasn't until she enrolled in her freshman year at the University of Central Oklahoma (at age 47) that her poetry began to deepen and truly express her great love for her Catholic faith. Her favorite poems are rhyming, story poems which weave around a person's thoughts and emotions. She says she writes with an Oklahoman's heart and accent.

Our Lady of Sorrows,
Pray for us.

www.ingramcontent.com/pod-product-compliance
Lightning Source LLC
Chambersburg PA
CBHW040348060426

42445CB00030B/155

9 780692 952603